9 Habits of Thriving Sole Proprietors: Mastering Success in Your Own Venture.

By

George C. Hall

9 Habits of Thriving Sole Proprietors: Mastering Success in Your Own Venture.

1

9 Habits of Thriving Sole Proprietors: Mastering Success in Your Own Venture.

2

INTRODUCTION

9 Habits of Thriving Sole Proprietors: Mastering Success in Your Own Venture.

3

In the ever-changing landscape of entrepreneurship, single proprietors serve as independent trailblazers, carving their own routes to economic success. These entrepreneurial individuals handle hurdles and capitalize on opportunities as lone adventurers in the world of trade with a distinctive blend of determination and resourcefulness.

A sole proprietor's journey is about living and conquering success in their own enterprise, not just survival. Certain behaviors arise as defining qualities of these thriving individuals in order to accomplish this feat. In this investigation, we will look at the nine key practices that distinguish thriving

9 Habits of Thriving Sole Proprietors: Mastering Success in Your Own Venture.

4

single entrepreneurs and pave the route for their success.

1st Habit: Visionary Clarity A crystal-clear vision is at the heart of every successful lone proprietor's journey. These business owners are skilled at imagining their company's future, creating goals, and charting a course to success. They build a purpose-driven enterprise that draws consumers, partners, and investors by continually connecting their activities with their mission.

Habit 2: Unyielding Self-Discipline Successful lone proprietors recognise the value of discipline. They have mastered

9 Habits of Thriving Sole Proprietors: Mastering Success in Your Own Venture.

5

the art of time management, prioritization, and sticking to a well-structured routine. This unwavering self-discipline enables them to stay focused on critical activities, avoid distractions, and maintain a high level of productivity even when faced with obstacles.

3rd Habit: Constant Learning Staying static in the fast-paced world of business is not an option. Successful sole proprietors are lifelong learners who are constantly looking for new knowledge and abilities to keep up with shifting trends and technologies. They recognise that pursuing knowledge is an

9 Habits of Thriving Sole Proprietors: Mastering Success in Your Own Venture.

6

investment in the long-term viability of their business.

Habit 4: Focus on the Customer Customers are at the center of the business for exceptional sole entrepreneurs. They pay close attention to their clients' demands, adjust their offerings to meet those needs, and give great service that creates long-term partnerships. This customer-centric strategy fosters not only customer loyalty but also word-of-mouth referrals.

5th Habit: Resilience in the Face of Adversity In the entrepreneurial path, setbacks and failures are unavoidable. Successful lone proprietors demonstrate

9 Habits of Thriving Sole Proprietors: Mastering Success in Your Own Venture.

7

resilience by viewing failures as learning experiences. They adapt, pivot, and devise novel methods to overcome obstacles, viewing adversity as a stepping stone to greater achievement.

6th Habit: Strategic Networking is the sixth most important habit. Networking is essential for sole proprietors' success. These business owners actively seek out opportunities to network with their colleagues, mentors, and possible partners. Their capacity to form meaningful relationships allows them to access a multitude of knowledge, resources, and support, which speeds up their growth.

9 Habits of Thriving Sole Proprietors: Mastering Success in Your Own Venture.

8

7th Habit: Embrace Innovation In a continuously changing business landscape, embracing innovation is a must. To keep ahead of the competition, successful sole owners are constantly exploring new technology, business strategies, and creative solutions. Because of their openness to experiment and adapt, they are positioned as industry leaders.

8th Habit: Financial Intelligence A successful solitary proprietorship is distinguished by sound financial management. They place a premium on financial literacy, meticulously analyzing costs, managing cash flow, and making sound investment selections. This

9 Habits of Thriving Sole Proprietors: Mastering Success in Your Own Venture.

9

financial expertise supports the venture's stability and sustainability.

9th Habit: Work-Life Balance While entrepreneurship requires commitment, successful lone proprietors recognise the value of work-life integration. They put their health first, striking a healthy balance between their professional and personal life. They stay energized and ready to tackle the hurdles of entrepreneurship by nourishing themselves.

We will go deeply into each of these nine habits that define the journey of thriving sole proprietors in the following exploration. We acquire insights into

9 Habits of Thriving Sole Proprietors: Mastering Success in Your Own Venture.

10

how great entrepreneurs master their distinct pathways in business by studying the tactics, mindsets, and practices that underpin their success.

These individuals serve as role models for all those embarking on the exhilarating adventure of sole proprietorship through their visionary clarity, self-discipline, continuous learning, customer-centric approach, resilience, strategic networking, innovation, financial acumen, and work-life integration. Join us as we learn the secrets to flourishing as a sole proprietor and mastering entrepreneurship success.

9 Habits of Thriving Sole Proprietors: Mastering Success in Your Own Venture.

11

CHAPTER 1.

DEVELOPING AN ENTREPRENEURIAL MIND SET.

Entrepreneurial mindset is a powerful and dynamic way of thinking and

9 Habits of Thriving Sole Proprietors: Mastering Success in Your Own Venture.

12

problem-solving that encourages people to recognise possibilities, take calculated risks, and develop
inventive solutions. It entails a distinct set of attitudes, behaviors, and habits that set entrepreneurs apart from the crowd.
In today's quickly changing business world, cultivating an entrepreneurial attitude is critical for success, not only for individuals looking to start their own businesses but also for intrapreneurs within established organizations.

The entrepreneurial attitude is defined at its foundation by a willingness to embrace uncertainty and ambiguity. Entrepreneurs are at ease venturing into the unknown, knowing that

9 Habits of Thriving Sole Proprietors: Mastering Success in Your Own Venture.

13

With risk comes reward. They are motivated by a desire to solve issues and add value, rather than being satisfied with the status quo. This drive propels their will to conquer challenges and persevere in the face of adversity.

The capacity to discover opportunities in unexpected places is an important part of the entrepreneurial mindset. Entrepreneurs have a strong eye for market gaps or unmet demands that others may miss. They are skilled in identifying trends, forecasting client preferences, and imagining creative products or services to fill these gaps. This mindset pushes people to seek out

9 Habits of Thriving Sole Proprietors: Mastering Success in Your Own Venture.

14

chances rather than waiting for them to come to them.

The entrepreneurial mindset is defined by its ability to innovate. Entrepreneurs are natural innovators who are always looking for new and better ways to accomplish things. They question assumptions, challenge norms, and push limits to

generate ideas that can disrupt industries or revolutionize procedures. This imaginative urge is frequently motivated by a desire to make a significant difference and leave a lasting legacy.

9 Habits of Thriving Sole Proprietors: Mastering Success in Your Own Venture.

15

Another aspect of the entrepreneurial mindset is a high sense of self-efficacy. Entrepreneurs think that their actions have the power to impact results. This self-assurance allows them to take the initiative, make decisions, and pivot as needed. Even when they fail, they see setbacks as chances for development and learning rather than insurmountable obstacles.

The entrepreneurial attitude requires adaptability and flexibility. Entrepreneurs must be willing to pivot their strategy and adapt to new conditions because the business landscape is continuously changing. This necessitates an openness to change as

9 Habits of Thriving Sole Proprietors: Mastering Success in Your Own Venture.

16

well as a proactive commitment to learning and development.

Networking and teamwork are also essential components of an entrepreneurial attitude. Entrepreneurs understand the importance of solid relationships with mentors, peers, investors, and customers.

These connections provide possibilities for feedback, support, and collaboration, all of which can increase the likelihood of success. Entrepreneurs can harness multiple perspectives and abilities through collaboration, resulting in more comprehensive and well-rounded solutions.

9 Habits of Thriving Sole Proprietors: Mastering Success in Your Own Venture.

17

Failure is an unavoidable aspect of the business journey, and the mindset necessary to recover from them is crucial. Failures are viewed as beneficial learning experiences by entrepreneurs rather than as evidence of weakness. This

resilience helps individuals to persevere in the face of adversity and to pursue their goals with unshakable determination.

Furthermore, entrepreneurs must have strong time management and prioritization abilities in order to negotiate the responsibilities of running a firm. With limited resources, they must

9 Habits of Thriving Sole Proprietors: Mastering Success in Your Own Venture.

18

focus their time and energy on high-impact projects that contribute to the growth of their businesses. Discipline and the capacity to say "no" to distractions that do not correspond with their goals are required.

The entrepreneurial attitude is built on education and ongoing learning. Entrepreneurs are eager learners that seek out information about their sector, market trends, and new technologies. This dedication to learning enables them to stay ahead of the competition and make sound business judgements.

To summarize, the entrepreneurial mindset is a complex and dynamic

9 Habits of Thriving Sole Proprietors: Mastering Success in Your Own Venture.

19

approach to problem-solving that fosters innovation, risk-taking, and the constant search of chances. It's a way of thinking that lives on ambiguity, is motivated by enthusiasm, and views failure as a stepping stone to achievement.

While not everyone is cut out to be an entrepreneur, fostering parts of the entrepreneurial mindset can lead to increased adaptability, resilience, and innovation in many facets of life and work. As the corporate landscape evolves, people that adopt this approach will be better positioned to navigate change, generate value, and leave a lasting impression.

9 Habits of Thriving Sole Proprietors: Mastering Success in Your Own Venture.

20

CHAPTER 2

9 Habits of Thriving Sole Proprietors: Mastering Success in Your Own Venture.

21

SETTING CLEAR GOALS AND STRATEGIES.

Setting specific Pretensions and strategies is a critical element of successful entrepreneurship. In a fast changing
company requests where competition is tough and coffers are scarce, having a well- defined roadmap becomes critical for attaining long- term success and prostrating obstacles.

This essay investigates the value of easily defined pretensions and strategies in entrepreneurship, diving into their advantages, major factors, and stylish practices.

9 Habits of Thriving Sole Proprietors: Mastering Success in Your Own Venture.

22

The significance of establishing specific pretensions and tactics.

Entrepreneurship is distinguished by its dynamic nature, which necessitates individualities navigating query, taking advised pitfalls, and continually conforming.

Clear pretensions and strategies act as guiding lights in such a setting, furnishing direction and purpose. Improve decision making, resource allocation, and performance evaluation for entrepreneurs. Clear pretensions give a feeling of attention, keeping entrepreneurs from being lost in the plethora of openings and diversions that arise. In discrepancy, well- defined plans specify the processes needed to attain

9 Habits of Thriving Sole Proprietors: Mastering Success in Your Own Venture.

23

these pretensions, icing that sweats are aligned with the anticipated issues.

THE BENEFITS OF SETTING SMART PRETENSIONS AND STRATEGIES

•More Focus and Alignment: Setting clear pretensions allows businesses to concentrate their sweats on what truly counts. When everyone in the organization knows the common pretensions, their conduct and opinions come
more aligned, producing a more cohesive and effective working terrain.
•Improved Decision- Making : Having predefined pretensions and tactics makes decision- making easier. Entrepreneurs

9 Habits of Thriving Sole Proprietors: Mastering Success in Your Own Venture.

24

can estimate results based on their capability to contribute to the defined pretensions, allowing them to make opinions that are more in line with the long- term vision.

•Dimension and Responsibility : Well-defined objects give quantitative criteria against which progress may be measured. This responsibility ensures that individual and platoon performance can be objectively analyzed, performing in ongoing development.

•Resource Allocation : Well- defined styles aid in the applicable allocation of coffers. Entrepreneurs can prioritize conditioning that is aligned with their points, avoiding squandering time and

9 Habits of Thriving Sole Proprietors: Mastering Success in Your Own Venture.

25

coffers on systems that don't add to the broader vision.

•Adaption and Inflexibility : While pretensions give direction, strategies give for prosecution inflexibility. Entrepreneurs can acclimatize their styles as circumstances change while keeping the larger points in mind, helping them to remain sensitive to request oscillations.

KEY RUDIMENTS OF DETERMINING CLEAR PRETENSIONS AND STRATEGIES .

•Specificity: pretensions should be specific, stating what has to be fulfilled.

9 Habits of Thriving Sole Proprietors: Mastering Success in Your Own Venture.

26

nebulous pretensions might lead to confusion and weakened sweats. particularity aids in task appreciation and prioritization.

•Measurability: pretensions must be measurable in order for entrepreneurs to measure their progress and success. Quantifiable criteria aid in assessing accomplishments and relating areas for development.

•Achievability: While lofty pretensions are desirable, they must also be attainable. Setting unrealistic prospects might lead to despondency and dissatisfaction. Pretensions should be grueling but not inviting.

•Applicability : pretensions must be harmonious with the overarching vision

9 Habits of Thriving Sole Proprietors: Mastering Success in Your Own Venture.

27

and charge of the company. inapplicable pretensions might deflect coffers down from what's authentically important to the business success.

•Time - bound : Giving pretensions and strategy deadlines adds urgency and organization. A schedule discourages procrastination and encourages steady trouble.

Stylish Practices for Establishing Specific Pretensions and Strategies.

•Visionary Clarity : Begin with a clear knowledge of the company's long- term vision.

9 Habits of Thriving Sole Proprietors: Mastering Success in Your Own Venture.

28

This vision acts as the pivot around which all other objects and tactics revolve.

•Breakdown Complexity: Break down the big picture vision into lower, more manageable pretensions. This regular fashion delivers a sense of success while also keeping provocation high.

•SMART pretensions : To develop pretensions, use the SMART(Specific, Measurable, Attainable, Applicable, Time- bound) frame. This ensures that pretensions are clear and attainable.

•Market Research: Conduct expansive request exploration in order to identify openings and challenges. This data-driven approach aids in the development

9 Habits of Thriving Sole Proprietors: Mastering Success in Your Own Venture.

29

of realistic pretensions and strategies that reverberate with the target followership.

•SWOT Analysis: Conduct a geek analysis
(Strengths, weaknesses, opportunities, time) to assess the internal and external surroundings of the business. This analysis helps with thing- setting by showing areas for development and prospective growth openings.

•Flexibility : While pretensions give guidance, keep open to altering plans in response to feedback and changing request circumstances. Inflexibility is needed to capitalize on imperative possibilities and overcome unexpected problems.

9 Habits of Thriving Sole Proprietors: Mastering Success in Your Own Venture.

30

•Communication and collaboration: Involve crucial stakeholders in things-setting communication and collaboration. Their views and shoes can help to ameliorate strategy expression and foster a sense of participating power.

Conclusion.

Setting defined pretensions and strategies is critical in the ever- changing geography of entrepreneurship. These tools help entrepreneurs manage hurdles and capitalize on openings by giving them direction, purpose, and a methodical

approach. Entrepreneurs can achieve long- term success and sustainable

9 Habits of Thriving Sole Proprietors: Mastering Success in Your Own Venture.

31

growth by perfecting their focus, decision- timber, and resource allocation.

Entrepreneurs can design a roadmap that directs their businesses towards their targeted issues by espousing stylish practices similar to visionary clarity, SMART thing setting, and rigidity.

The significance of clear pretensions and plans remains a vital asset in reaching greatness as the entrepreneurial trip evolves.

9 Habits of Thriving Sole Proprietors: Mastering Success in Your Own Venture.

32

CHAPTER 3 .

EFFECTIVE TIME MANAGEMENT.

Effective time management is a necessary skill for entrepreneurs attempting to navigate the fast-paced and demanding business scene. Time is a limited resource, and how an entrepreneur manages it can have a huge impact on his or her success. This article dives into several time management tactics and approaches that entrepreneurs

9 Habits of Thriving Sole Proprietors: Mastering Success in Your Own Venture.

33

can use to improve their productivity. The tactics are as follows;

•Establishing Clear Goals and Priorities: Entrepreneurs should begin by establishing clear and attainable goals. These objectives serve as the cornerstone for good time management, giving everyday activities direction and purpose. Entrepreneurs should focus on incremental progress by dividing down larger ambitions into

smaller, doable activities. Prioritization is essential; entrepreneurs should select tasks that

9 Habits of Thriving Sole Proprietors: Mastering Success in Your Own Venture.

34

match with their long-term goals and have a greater impact on the growth of their business.

•The Eisenhower Matrix: The Eisenhower Matrix is a common technique for prioritization that divides work into four quadrants: Urgent and Important, Important but Not Urgent, Urgent but Not Important, and Neither Urgent nor Important. This matrix assists entrepreneurs in distinguishing between tasks that must be completed immediately and those that may be scheduled or delegated.

•Time Blocking: Allocating particular blocks of time for distinct jobs or

9 Habits of Thriving Sole Proprietors: Mastering Success in Your Own Venture.

35

activities is known as time blocking. Entrepreneurs may guarantee that they commit sufficient time to high-priority work while avoiding multitasking and distractions by segmenting the day into

designated time slots. This strategy improves concentration and productivity.

•The Pomodoro Technique: The Pomodoro Technique recommends dividing work into focused intervals of 25 minutes, followed by a short break. A lengthier pause is taken after completing a certain number of intervals. This method takes advantage of the brain's ability to concentrate for shorter periods of time and can help prevent burnout.

9 Habits of Thriving Sole Proprietors: Mastering Success in Your Own Venture.

36

•Delegation and Outsourcing: Entrepreneurs frequently wear many hats, yet effective time management requires understanding when to assign duties. Delegating work to team members or outsourcing non-core activities enables entrepreneurs to focus on high-value tasks that have a direct impact on the success of their organization.

•Eliminating Time Wasters: It is critical to identify and eliminate time-wasting behaviors. Entrepreneurs should evaluate and reduce or eliminate activities that do not contribute to their aims. This could include cutting back on social

9 Habits of Thriving Sole Proprietors: Mastering Success in Your Own Venture.

37

media, streamlining meetings, and decreasing superfluous administrative work.

•Technology and Tools: Using technology and productivity tools can improve time management dramatically. Collaboration is streamlined and everyone is on the same page thanks to project management software, task tracking apps, and communication tools. Tools for automation can also handle monotonous jobs, freeing up time for more strategic endeavors.

•The 2-Minute Rule: According to entrepreneur and author David Allen, if a

9 Habits of Thriving Sole Proprietors: Mastering Success in Your Own Venture.

38

task can be finished in two minutes or less, it should bc completed right away. This keeps minor jobs from piling up and becoming burdensome.

•Maintaining Work-Life Balance: Effective time management comprises more than just professional activities; it also includes personal well-being. Entrepreneurs must prioritize their

own well-being and make time for family, hobbies, and recreation. Work-life balance is critical since burnout can stifle productivity and innovation.

9 Habits of Thriving Sole Proprietors: Mastering Success in Your Own Venture.

39

•Review and Adaptation: Entrepreneurs should evaluate the effectiveness of their time management techniques on a regular basis. Priorities and goals change as the business landscape changes. Being adaptive and willing

to improve time management approaches guarantees that efficiency is maintained.

•Learning to Say No: Entrepreneurs must master the art of saying no. While opportunities can be appealing, not all of them coincide with the aims of an entrepreneur. Overcommitment is avoided by politely accepting duties or projects that divert from the fundamental objective of the organization.

9 Habits of Thriving Sole Proprietors: Mastering Success in Your Own Venture.

40

•Mindfulness and Mindset: Being completely present in each task is part of a thoughtful

approach to time management. Mindfulness decreases the likelihood of distractions and enhances work quality. Furthermore, establishing a growth mentality encourages entrepreneurs to see problems as learning opportunities, which leads to better time management skills.

To summarize, good time management is a critical component of entrepreneurial success. Entrepreneurs can optimize their use of time by creating clear goals,

9 Habits of Thriving Sole Proprietors: Mastering Success in Your Own Venture.

41

prioritizing tasks, employing strategies such as the Eisenhower Matrix and time blocking, delegating, removing time wasters, exploiting technology, and preserving work-life balance.

Regular assessment and adaptation, combined with a growth-oriented mindset, contribute to increased efficiency and attainment of corporate objectives. In a world where time is a valuable commodity, mastering time management is more than a skill; it's a competitive edge.

9 Habits of Thriving Sole Proprietors: Mastering Success in Your Own Venture.

42

CHAPTER 4.

FINANCIAL SAVVINESS AND BUDGETING.

Financial savvy and smart planning are essential components in the field of entrepreneurship that can decide a venture's success or failure. Whether

9 Habits of Thriving Sole Proprietors: Mastering Success in Your Own Venture.

43

you're starting a new business or running an old one, understanding financial fundamentals and being able to construct and manage a budget may make a huge impact on your company's growth and sustainability. We'll go into the necessity of financial savvy and budgeting, the critical steps to developing these skills, and the possible rewards they can offer to your entrepreneurial journey in this detailed exploration.

THE IMPORTANCE OF FINANCIAL SKILL.

Financial savvy is the ability to understand, analyze, and manage a company's financial elements. Making

9 Habits of Thriving Sole Proprietors: Mastering Success in Your Own Venture.

44

informed decisions based on a thorough understanding of financial accounts, cash flow, and investment prospects is required. Financially knowledgeable entrepreneurs are capable of navigating economic uncertainty, making strategic financial decisions, and optimizing their resources.

The inherent risk of beginning and growing a firm is one of the key reasons financial savvy is essential in entrepreneurship. Without a sound financial basis, businesses are more likely to overspend, misallocate resources, and fail to anticipate cash flow issues. Entrepreneurs that are financially knowledgeable can reduce

9 Habits of Thriving Sole Proprietors: Mastering Success in Your Own Venture.

45

risks, find chances for growth, and assure long-term stability.

•The Budgeting Art:
Budgeting is the process of developing a plan that describes how a company's resources will be allocated over a specified time period. This includes assessing revenues, forecasting expenses, and establishing specific financial targets. A well-structured budget acts as a road map that guides decision-making, aids in resource allocation, and allows financial progress to be tracked.

Due to limited resources, unstable markets, and the need for rigorous

9 Habits of Thriving Sole Proprietors: Mastering Success in Your Own Venture.

46

financial management, budgeting is especially critical in entrepreneurship. A well-planned budget allows entrepreneurs to devote finances to essential areas such as product development, marketing, and operating expenses, all while leaving room for unforeseen circumstances.

IMPROVING FINANCIAL SKILLS AND BUDGETING SKILLS.

Education and trainingThe first step is to understand financial concepts. Entrepreneurs can create a strong foundation of financial knowledge by taking online courses, attending

9 Habits of Thriving Sole Proprietors: Mastering Success in Your Own Venture.

47

workshops, or even pursuing formal schooling in finance.

•Financial Reports: Entrepreneurs should learn to understand and interpret financial statements including the balance sheet, income statement, and cash flow statement. These records reveal information about a company's financial condition.

•Cash Flow Management : Understanding cash flow management is critical. To guarantee that the business remains solvent, entrepreneurs should understand the timing of income and expenses.

•Investment Strategy : Astute business owners evaluate investment

9 Habits of Thriving Sole Proprietors: Mastering Success in Your Own Venture.

48

opportunities, whether in new initiatives, technologics, or markets, with a clear grasp of prospective returns and dangers.

•Risk Management : It is critical to understand and manage financial risks. This includes diversifying revenue streams, having backup plans, and possibly using insurance.

•Networking: Connecting with financial professionals, mentors, and peers can provide useful insights and viewpoints on financial decisions.

•Technology : Financial software and tools make planning and financial tracking easier. These solutions can provide real-time information about cash flow and expenses.

9 Habits of Thriving Sole Proprietors: Mastering Success in Your Own Venture.

49

BENEFITS OF FINANCIAL INTELLIGENCE AND BUDGETING

•Strategic Determination: Entrepreneurs that are financially knowledgeable make informed judgements that are in line with the company's overall goals and financial capabilities.

•Resource Optimisation : Effective budgeting ensures that resources are efficiently allocated, eliminating waste and improving profitability.

•Risk Reduction : Entrepreneurs should anticipate obstacles and take proactive efforts to mitigate their impact by comprehending financial risks.

9 Habits of Thriving Sole Proprietors: Mastering Success in Your Own Venture.

50

•Investor Satisfaction: Financial competence can create trust in potential investors, partners, and stakeholders, leading to increased funding opportunities.

•Long-Term Sustainability: Entrepreneurs that prioritize financial acumen and budgeting are more likely to achieve long-term business viability and growth.

•Adaptability : Entrepreneurs with a sound financial basis can better navigate economic downturns or market volatility.

Finally, financial acumen and budgeting are essential abilities for entrepreneurs

9 Habits of Thriving Sole Proprietors: Mastering Success in Your Own Venture.

51

seeking to build and expand profitable enterprises. Understanding financial principles, creating effective budgets, and making informed decisions may all have a significant impact on the course of a business.

Entrepreneurs may develop robust and thriving firms that stand the test of time by investing in financial knowledge, embracing budgeting practices, and constantly honing these abilities

CHAPTER 5

9 Habits of Thriving Sole Proprietors: Mastering Success in Your Own Venture.

52

BUILDING A STRONG ONLINE PRESENCE.

In moment's digital world, having a strong online presence is essential for both individuals and businesses. Because the internet is now the primary venue for communication, networking, and marketing, developing a strong online presence may have a substantial impact on particular branding, professional achievement, and business growth.

This essay digs into the ways and important factors that contribute to the development of an important online presence.

9 Habits of Thriving Sole Proprietors: Mastering Success in Your Own Venture.

53

COMPREHENDING ONLINE PRESENCE.

The digital footmark that an individual or organization leaves on the internet is pertained to as an online presence. It includes a wide range of aspects, similar as social media biographies, websites, blogs, vids, podcasts, and any other digital platforms where a followership can interact. A strong online presence not only allows you to reach a larger followership, but it also promotes credibility, trust, and engagement.

1. Creating a Reliable Brand Identity : A strong online presence begins with a distinct brand identity. thickness in

9 Habits of Thriving Sole Proprietors: Mastering Success in Your Own Venture.

54

branding is vital whether you're an individual professional or a marketable reality. This entails utilizing harmonious color schemes, ensigns, and tone of voice across all internet channels. thickness aids in the development of recognition and trust among your target followership.

2. Produce a stoner-Friendly Website : A well- designed website is the foundation of an important online presence. It should be visually beautiful, simple to use, and mobile-friendly. Your website should deliver applicable and precious information that addresses your target

9 Habits of Thriving Sole Proprietors: Mastering Success in Your Own Venture.

55

followership's conditions and interests. Streamlining your website with new content on a regular basis improves its hunt machine visibility.

3. Creating Engaging Content : Any successful internet presence relies on high- quality content. Content, whether in the form of blog papers, vids, infographics, or podcasts, should be educational, applicable, and intriguing. advertisement on a regular base helps to keep your followership interested and informed.

4. Mastery of Social Media : Social media platforms are effective tools for establishing and sustaining an online

9 Habits of Thriving Sole Proprietors: Mastering Success in Your Own Venture.

56

presence select platforms that correspond to the preferences and demographics of your target followership. Share information on a regular basis, interact with your followers, and take part in important exchanges. Each platform necessitates a distinct strategy, so customize your material consequently.

5. SEO(Search Machine Optimisation) : SEO is necessary for adding your internet visibility. By optimizing your website and content with applicable keywords, meta markers, and high-quality reverse links, you boost the liability of hunt machines discovering your content. Good organic business to

9 Habits of Thriving Sole Proprietors: Mastering Success in Your Own Venture.

57

your online platforms is a result of good hunt machine rankings.

6. Collaboration and Networking : Uniting with others in your business or area might boost your internet profile dramatically. unite with influencers, blogs, or businesses who partake your heartstrings. Guest advertisement, cooperative webinars, and social media appropriations are each great styles to connect with their followership and broaden your reach.

7. Interaction and Engagement : Erecting a great online presence entails further than just propagating content; it also entails cultivating connections. Respond

9 Habits of Thriving Sole Proprietors: Mastering Success in Your Own Venture.

58

to commentary, textbooks, and emails as soon as possible. Demonstrate genuine interest in your followership's studies and feedback. This position of participation develops a sense of belonging and trust.

8. Paid Promotion and Online Advertising : While organic development is pivotal, employing online advertising can significantly increase your reach. Platforms similar as Google Advertisements and social network advertisements enable you to target certain demographics, adding your chances of reaching the intended followership.

9 Habits of Thriving Sole Proprietors: Mastering Success in Your Own Venture.

59

9.   Monitoring   and   Evaluation: Monitoring the success of your online presence on a regular basis is critical for making informed opinions. Track website business, social media commerce, and content performance with analytics tools. To optimize your presence, acclimate your strategies grounded on the perceptivity acquired.

10. Trends and Technology Adaptation : The digital geography is ever- changing, with new trends and technology appearing on a regular basis. It's critical to stay up to date on these changes and alter your styles consequently in order to retain a strong online presence. Accept new platforms and tools that are in line

9 Habits of Thriving Sole Proprietors: Mastering Success in Your Own Venture.

60

with your objects and followership preferences.

Conclusion A good online presence is a vital tool in the digital age for individuals and businesses seeking to make credibility, attract a larger followership, and achieve their pretensions.

You can construct an important online presence that opens up a world of openings and success by developing a harmonious brand identity, furnishing compelling content, understanding social media, and staying on top of new trends. Flash back that developing your online presence is a continual process that demands attention, creativity, and

9 Habits of Thriving Sole Proprietors: Mastering Success in Your Own Venture.

61

constant adoption in order to remain applicable in an ever- changing digital geography.

CHAPTER 6

CUSTOMER-CENTRIC APPROACH.

A customer-centric approach to entrepreneurship centers on putting consumers' wants, preferences,
and satisfaction at the center of business strategy. In a world where customer

9 Habits of Thriving Sole Proprietors: Mastering Success in Your Own Venture.

62

choices are broad and competition is severe, such an approach is not only an option, but a requirement for long-term prosperity. This essay examines the relevance, benefits, techniques, and problems of a customer-centric strategy in entrepreneurship.

Importance : In today's commercial world, customers carry enormous power. Their feedback may make or destroy a company, and their loyalty can lead to constant cash sources.

A customer-centric approach recognises this effect and strives to create a company model based on knowing and responding to their needs. Businesses that focus on client needs can build

9 Habits of Thriving Sole Proprietors: Mastering Success in Your Own Venture.

63

products and services that truly resonate, generating brand loyalty and positive word-of-mouth.

BENEFITS:

•Increased Customer Satisfaction : A company that prioritizes its clients develops a reputation for providing value. Meeting or exceeding client expectations results in higher satisfaction and repeat business.

•Loyalty and retention have increased : Customers are more likely to remain loyal to a brand when they feel respected and heard. Loyal customers not only contribute to consistent revenue, but they

9 Habits of Thriving Sole Proprietors: Mastering Success in Your Own Venture.

64

also serve as brand ambassadors, driving new client acquisition.

•Better Innovation : Businesses acquire insights into their consumers' pain points and objectives

by connecting with them intimately. This data feeds innovation, allowing entrepreneurs to develop products and services that address real-world problems.

•Advantage in Competition : A customer-centric approach can set a company apart from its competition. Businesses that succeed at understanding

9 Habits of Thriving Sole Proprietors: Mastering Success in Your Own Venture.

65

and serving their consumers frequently gain a market advantage.

•Increased Revenue and Growth : Happy customers are more likely to spend money and suggest a brand. This, in turn, increases revenue and allows for corporate expansion.

STRATEGIES:

•Customer Research : Conduct extensive market research to learn about customer preferences, behaviors, and problem concerns. This can be

accomplished through the use of surveys, focus groups, and data analysis.

9 Habits of Thriving Sole Proprietors: Mastering Success in Your Own Venture.

66

•Pcrsonalization : Tailor products and services to match the demands of each individual customer. Offering customization choices or making personalized recommendations could be examples of this.

•Successful Communication : Maintain open channels of communication with your customers. Respond to inquiries, feedback, and concerns as soon as possible. Seek input actively in order to develop continuously.

•Presence on Multiple Channels : Engage clients where they are most comfortable by being available across

9 Habits of Thriving Sole Proprietors: Mastering Success in Your Own Venture.

67

numerous platforms and channels. Social media, websites, mobile apps, and physical storefronts are all examples of this.

•Employee Development : Instruct staff on how to prioritize client demands and give great service. Employees that recognise the value of client pleasure serve as brand ambassadors.

•Ongoing Improvement : Based on client input, analyze and improve your products, services, and procedures on a regular basis. Adapt to evolving market conditions and client preferences.

CHALLENGES :

9 Habits of Thriving Sole Proprietors: Mastering Success in Your Own Venture.

68

•How to Balance Diverse Customer Needs: Customers have a wide range of preferences, and catering to them all might be difficult. It is critical to strike a balance between customisation and scalability.

•Problems with Data Privacy : Collecting client data for personalisation can generate privacy and

data security concerns. Businesses must be upfront about data usage and adhere to all applicable legislation.

•Allocation of Resources: Implementing a customer-centric approach necessitates

9 Habits of Thriving Sole Proprietors: Mastering Success in Your Own Venture.

69

a financial, time, and effort investment. It may be difficult for startups and small firms to deploy resources effectively.

•Evolution of Customer Expectations : Customer tastes can shift quickly, making it challenging for firms to stay current. Staying on top of these changes is critical for long-term success.

•Internal Alignment : It can be difficult to ensure that the entire organization, from leadership to frontline personnel, is aligned with a customer-centric vision.

Conclusion.
A customer-centric approach is more than a catchphrase; it represents a

9 Habits of Thriving Sole Proprietors: Mastering Success in Your Own Venture.

70

fundamental transformation in how firms operate. Entrepreneurs that put their customers first are better positioned to respond to market changes, create long-term connections, and achieve sustainable growth.

While there are hurdles, the benefits of such a strategy, such as increased satisfaction, loyalty, and innovation, greatly exceed the drawbacks.

A customer-centric approach is a guiding principle that can guide firms to long-term success in the ever-changing world of entrepreneurship.

9 Habits of Thriving Sole Proprietors: Mastering Success in Your Own Venture.

71

CHAPTER 7

9 Habits of Thriving Sole Proprietors: Mastering Success in Your Own Venture.

72

NETWORKING AND COLLABORATIONS.

Collaboration and networking are critical components of success in a variety of fields, including business, education, and personal activities. In today's quickly changing world, the capacity to connect with others, share ideas, and collaborate towards common goals is becoming increasingly important.

This article discusses the relevance of networking and collaborations, as well as their benefits and strategies for properly using their potential.

•The Networking Advantage:

9 Habits of Thriving Sole Proprietors: Mastering Success in Your Own Venture.

73

Building and maintaining ties with others who have similar interests, aspirations, or sectors is what networking entails. It acts as a forum for the exchange of knowledge, experiences, and possibilities. Networking, whether professional or personal, builds ties that can lead to both immediate and long-term rewards.

•Professional Benefits:
Networking provides several professional benefits. It can lead to new work prospects, career progression, and industry knowledge. Individuals can meet experts, potential mentors, and peers by attending conferences, seminars, and workshops. These contacts

9 Habits of Thriving Sole Proprietors: Mastering Success in Your Own Venture.

74

can lead to unadvertised job opportunities and important carccr guidance. Furthermore, networking allows professionals to stay up to date on the newest trends and advances in their domains by facilitating the exchange of best practices.

•Business Expansion:
Networking is a critical component of corporate growth. Collaboration with complementary businesses might result in collaborations that increase client base and improve products. Companies may strengthen their supply chain and gain a competitive advantage by engaging with suppliers, distributors, and even competitors.

9 Habits of Thriving Sole Proprietors: Mastering Success in Your Own Venture.

75

Networking also allows entrepreneurs to obtain money from investors, accelerators, and venture capitalists, hence promoting the growth of startups and creative companies.

•Knowledge Exchange:
Networking opens the door to knowledge sharing. Engaging with people from various backgrounds and industries exposes us to new perspectives and ideas. This cross-pollination of ideas can result in inventive solutions to problems and stimulate innovation. Collaborations among specialists from many fields have resulted in game-changing advances in science, technology, and the arts.

9 Habits of Thriving Sole Proprietors: Mastering Success in Your Own Venture.

76

•Personal Advancement:

Networking isn't just for professional advancement; it also helps with personal development. Engaging in meaningful interactions with a diverse range of people can help to build communication skills, self-confidence, and interpersonal relationships. Individuals can be introduced to mentors and role models through networking, who can provide direction and support in both personal and professional aspects of life.

THE ADVANTAGES OF COLLABORATION.

9 Habits of Thriving Sole Proprietors: Mastering Success in Your Own Venture.

77

Collaborations include people or organizations working together to achieve a common goal. These collaborations can produce major benefits that may not be possible while working alone.

•Increased Creativity:
Brainstorming and idea-sharing sessions are common in collaborations. This interchange of ideas from various points of view can result in more imaginative and creative solutions. Collaborators can encourage one another to think beyond the box and investigate new alternatives.

•Common Resources:

9 Habits of Thriving Sole Proprietors: Mastering Success in Your Own Venture.

78

Collaborations have a significant advantage in terms of resource pooling. Collaborations, whether through the sharing of equipment, experience, or financial support, can enable access to assets that would not have been available otherwise. This pool of pooled resources can result in cost savings and more effective project execution.

•Risk Reduction:
Collaborations can assist in mitigating project risks. The likelihood of unexpected issues diminishes when numerous parties contribute their skills, experience, and resources.

9 Habits of Thriving Sole Proprietors: Mastering Success in Your Own Venture.

79

If one partner encounters difficulties, the others can step in to provide assistance and keep the project on schedule.

•Quicker Progress:
Working alone can result in slower progress owing to a lack of resources or knowledge gaps. Collaborations allow participants to distribute tasks among themselves, resulting in faster and more efficient project completion. Furthermore, collaborators can use one other's abilities to handle different elements of a project at the same time.

•Broadened Network:
Collaborations connect people to a larger network of contacts. Collaborators

9 Habits of Thriving Sole Proprietors: Mastering Success in Your Own Venture.

80

frequently build new connections through working closely with others, which might lead to additional chances in the future.

These ties can go beyond the current endeavor and form a web of partnerships that will continue to bear fruit in the future.

EFFECTIVE NETWORKING AND COLLABORATION STRATEGIES.

To get the most out of networking and collaborations, approach them carefully and thoughtfully. Consider the following strategies:

•Set specific objectives:

9 Habits of Thriving Sole Proprietors: Mastering Success in Your Own Venture.

81

It's critical to clarify your goals before plunging into networking or collaborations. Determine what you want to get out of these interactions. Clear goals will guide your efforts and help you stay focused, whether you're looking for a mentor, a new career, or establishing a joint project.

•Establish Genuine Relationships:
When relationships are established on authenticity and mutual respect, networking is most effective. Rather of perceiving individuals as possible stepping stones, approach networking with a genuine desire to learn from and encourage others. Genuine connections

9 Habits of Thriving Sole Proprietors: Mastering Success in Your Own Venture.

82

are more likely to provide substantial and long-term results.

•Make use of online platforms:
Online platforms have broadened the breadth of networking and partnerships in the digital age. Social media, professional networking sites, and online forums allow you to connect with people all over the world. Make the most of these platforms to expand your network and connect with experts that share your interests.

•Look for Collaborators Who Can Help You:

9 Habits of Thriving Sole Proprietors: Mastering Success in Your Own Venture.

83

When exploring collaborations, seek out partners with complementary talents and expertise. Collaborators with diverse skills sets can improve the overall quality of the project and result in more well-rounded outcomes.

•Effective Communication:
Communication must be clear and transparent in both networking and collaboration. Be open about your expectations, communicate your opinions freely, and actively listen to others' perspectives. Effective communication builds trust and keeps everyone on the same page.

9 Habits of Thriving Sole Proprietors: Mastering Success in Your Own Venture.

84

•Be Willing to Learn:

Networking and collaboration allow you to learn from others. Approach these discussions with an open mind and a commitment to learn and improve your skills. Be open to new ideas and techniques, even if they contradict your pre-existing beliefs.

•Take and Give:

A balance of giving and taking is required for successful networking and collaboration. Contribute your knowledge, thoughts, and resources to help others, and be open to receive aid when it is offered. This reciprocity lays a solid foundation for long-term relationships.

9 Habits of Thriving Sole Proprietors: Mastering Success in Your Own Venture.

85

Conclusion

Networking and collaboration are essential tools for personal and professional development. They allow us to connect with like-minded people, harness pooled resources, and achieve goals that might otherwise be out of our reach. Individuals and corporations may unleash a world of opportunity, stimulate innovation, and make meaningful contributions to their respective professions by embracing the power of networking and cooperation.

So, whether you're attending a networking event or embarking on a joint project,

9 Habits of Thriving Sole Proprietors: Mastering Success in Your Own Venture.

86

keep in mind that when we work together and have strong relationships, our chances of success multiply.

CHAPTER 8

9 Habits of Thriving Sole Proprietors: Mastering Success in Your Own Venture.

87

CONTINUOUS LEARNING AND SKILL DEVELOPMENT.

Concepts that have gained traction in today's fast-paced environment. In a world marked by technology breakthroughs, economic transformations, and shifting employment needs, the concept of gaining and improving skills has become critical for personal and professional development.

This essay goes into the relevance of continual learning, its advantages, and effective skill development tactics.

THE IMPORTANCE OF LIFELONG LEARNING.

9 Habits of Thriving Sole Proprietors: Mastering Success in Your Own Venture.

88

Continuous learning refers to the lifelong process of obtaining new knowledge, skills, and competences. It is a proactive approach to remaining relevant in a world where the only constant is change. Traditionally, education was associated with formal schools and degrees. However, the current world necessitates a paradigm shift towards a lifelong learning mindset.

The internet, in particular, has democratized access to information and learning resources. This has changed the way people study, allowing them to explore new topics and develop skills outside of traditional educational institutions. Because of the quick speed of technological progress, skills might

9 Habits of Thriving Sole Proprietors: Mastering Success in Your Own Venture.

89

become obsolete in a short amount of time. Individuals that engage in continuous learning can keep ahead of these changes and remain adaptive.

THE ADVANTAGES OF CONTINUOUS LEARNING.

•Professional Development : Ongoing learning improves one's job possibilities. Individuals that invest in their professional development are more likely to be considered for promotions, new employment possibilities, and leadership positions.

•Adaptability : The ability to constantly learn encourages adaptability. Individuals who can swiftly acquire and

9 Habits of Thriving Sole Proprietors: Mastering Success in Your Own Venture.

90

use new abilities are better positioned to overcome problems and exploit opportunities in a dynamic work environment.

•Innovation : Learning from many fields and disciplines can lead to idea cross-pollination. This frequently results in novel solutions to challenging challenges, which contribute to personal and organizational development.

•Confidence and Motivation : Learning new talents enhances one's self-esteem and motivation. Individuals' overall sense of success grows as they see themselves making progress and mastering new areas.

Engaging in learning activities stimulates cognitive functions and keeps the brain

9 Habits of Thriving Sole Proprietors: Mastering Success in Your Own Venture.

91

engaged. Lifelong learning has been related to a lower incidence of cognitive decline and better mental health.

•Networking : Pursuing lifelong learning frequently entails networking with peers, mentors, and experts. These contacts may lead to lucrative future collaborations and possibilities.

EFFECTIVE SKILL DEVELOPMENT STRATEGIES.

•Set Specific Learning Objectives : Establish specific learning objectives. Determine which talents are compatible with your personal and professional goals. This clarity will assist you in prioritizing and staying focused.

9 Habits of Thriving Sole Proprietors: Mastering Success in Your Own Venture.

92

•Embrace Curiosity : Develop a curious mentality. Be willing to investigate topics that may not be directly related to your current position. Curiosity fuels a desire to learn.

•Make Use of Online tools : The internet has a multitude of learning tools, including online courses, tutorials, podcasts, and webinars. Coursera, edX, Khan Academy, and LinkedIn Learning all offer a wide range of topics.

•Structured Learning Plans : Make a plan for skill learning that is structured. Break complicated skills down into smaller, more accessible sub-skills. This method simplifies learning and fosters a sense of success.

9 Habits of Thriving Sole Proprietors: Mastering Success in Your Own Venture.

93

•Practice and Application : Simply learning a skill is insufficient; regular practice is required for mastery. Apply what you've learned in class to real-world scenarios to cement your understanding.

•Feedback and Reflection : Seek feedback from mentors, peers, or field experts. Constructive criticism can help you improve your talents. Reflect on your progress on a regular basis and find opportunities for growth.

•Networking and Collaboration : Participate in communities that are connected to your areas of interest. Participate in online forums, meetups, and workshops. Collaboration with

9 Habits of Thriving Sole Proprietors: Mastering Success in Your Own Venture.

94

others improves learning by providing alternative views.

•Time Management : Set aside time for learning. Establishing a regimen that allows you to make consistent improvement is essential.

•Experimentation : Don't be scared to move outside of your comfort zone and try new things. Accepting failure as a necessary part of the learning process can provide significant insights.

Conclusion.

Finally, constant learning and skill development have become critical techniques for navigating the modern world's obstacles and opportunities.

9 Habits of Thriving Sole Proprietors: Mastering Success in Your Own Venture.

95

Adopting a lifelong learning mentality not only promotes personal and professional development, but it also promotes adaptability, inventiveness, and cognitive well-being.

Individuals now have unprecedented access to knowledge and skills thanks to the abundance of resources available. Individuals may continuously adapt and succeed in a fast changing landscape by defining clear goals,
remaining interested, and implementing effective learning practices.

9 Habits of Thriving Sole Proprietors: Mastering Success in Your Own Venture.

96

CHAPTER 9.

WORK-LIFE BALANCE AND SELF-CARE.

The search for a harmonious work-life balance and the practice of self-care have become key components of a meaningful

9 Habits of Thriving Sole Proprietors: Mastering Success in Your Own Venture.

97

and sustainable existence in today's fast-paced and demanding society.

Individuals are faced with the issue of dedicating time and energy to both professional responsibilities and personal well-being when the lines between work and personal life blur. This essay dives into the significance of work-life balance and self-care, examining the advantages, implementation tactics, and changing dynamics in the current world.

The Importance of Work-Life Balance:

Work-life balance refers to the balance of time and effort spent on one's

9 Habits of Thriving Sole Proprietors: Mastering Success in Your Own Venture.

98

professional and personal endeavors. A balanced approach

recognises the value of cultivating relationships, engaging in hobbies, preserving physical health, and dealing with stress. It recognises that an individual's well-being extends beyond the workplace and includes mental, emotional, and physical components. Obtaining this balance has various advantages.

For starters, a healthy work-life balance boosts productivity and job happiness. Individuals who schedule time for rest and relaxation return to work revitalized, resulting in enhanced focus, creativity,

9 Habits of Thriving Sole Proprietors: Mastering Success in Your Own Venture.

99

and overall performance. Furthermore, a healthy work-life balance decreases burnout and stress, promoting mental well-being. Chronic stress, which is frequently caused by extended work hours and disregard of personal life, can result in unfavorable health effects and lower job satisfaction.

The Importance of Self-Care:

Work-life balance is supplemented by self-care, which emphasizes the intentional practice of activities that improve general well-being. This includes a variety of elements such as physical, emotional, social, and psychological well-being. Self-care

9 Habits of Thriving Sole Proprietors: Mastering Success in Your Own Venture.

100

entails identifying one's own needs and committing time and resources to meet them. This could include practicing relaxation techniques, indulging in hobbies, eating a nutritious diet, exercising frequently, and obtaining emotional assistance when necessary.

Self-care is a necessity, not an indulgence. Prioritizing self-care gives people the resilience they need to face life's obstacles. It improves mental health by lowering anxiety and depression symptoms, improves physical health, and promotes a good self-image. Self-care

9 Habits of Thriving Sole Proprietors: Mastering Success in Your Own Venture.

101

practitioners are more suited to manage stress and maintain a healthier work-life balance.

Implementation Strategies:

Work-life balance and self-care take deliberate effort and smart preparation. Individuals can use the following ways to achieve these objectives:

•Establish limits : Define clear limits between work and personal life. Define and keep to set work hours, allowing yourself to disengage and recuperate during leisure time.

•Prioritize Tasks : Use time management skills to efficiently prioritize tasks. Identify and complete key work during

9 Habits of Thriving Sole Proprietors: Mastering Success in Your Own Venture.

102

peak productivity hours, leaving time for relaxing later.

•Use Time Blocking : Set aside defined blocks of time for work responsibilities, personal

activities, and self-care. This keeps work from invading personal time and vice versa.

•Unplug : To eliminate distractions and promote relaxation, limit the usage of digital gadgets during personal time.

•Exercise on a Regular Basis : Physical activity not only benefits physical health

9 Habits of Thriving Sole Proprietors: Mastering Success in Your Own Venture.

103

but also releases endorphins, which can reduce stress and boost mood.

•Nurture interactions : Make time for meaningful interactions with family and friends. Outside of work, strong social connections provide emotional support and improve life.

•Explore Hobbies : Engage in activities and interests that bring you joy and relaxation. Activities that you are enthusiastic about might

serve as a creative outlet and add to overall pleasure.

9 Habits of Thriving Sole Proprietors: Mastering Success in Your Own Venture.

104

•Practice Mindfulness : Mindfulness techniques like meditation and deep breathing can help you manage stress and focus better.

Prioritize work and obligations while learning to say no. Refuse new obligations that may overburden your calendar.

•Seek Professional Assistance: If stress or mental health issues become overwhelming, don't be afraid to seek professional assistance from therapists or counselors.

The Modern Landscape Is Evolving Dynamics:

9 Habits of Thriving Sole Proprietors: Mastering Success in Your Own Venture.

105

With cultural changes and technology improvements, the concept of work-life balance and self-care has developed. Individuals now have more control over their work settings thanks to the rise of remote work and flexible schedule possibilities. It has, however, blurred the barriers between business and home life, needing cautious boundary-setting.

Furthermore, the introduction of social media and continual connectedness has created new problems for self-care. The pressure to maintain a perfect online profile, as well as the fear of missing out (FOMO), can stymie genuine self-care attempts. Finding a happy medium between digital involvement and

9 Habits of Thriving Sole Proprietors: Mastering Success in Your Own Venture.

106

unplugging is now an essential component of well-rounded self-care.

Conclusion:
Work-life balance and self-care are not passing fads, but rather persistent ideals that lead to a balanced and fulfilled living.

Prioritizing these factors promotes not only individual well-being but also productivity, relationships, and overall life pleasure.

Individuals can negotiate the difficulties of life with resilience, purpose, and contentment by embracing the tactics suggested in this essay and adjusting to

9 Habits of Thriving Sole Proprietors: Mastering Success in Your Own Venture.

107

the developing dynamics of the modern world.

SUMMARY AND CONCLUSION.

The thorough guide "9 Habits of Thriving Sole Proprietors: Mastering Success in Your Own Venture" provides light on the main habits and tactics used by successful sole proprietors to succeed in their entrepreneurial journeys. This book gives useful insights and concrete recommendations for anyone wishing to build and sustain their own endeavors through a detailed examination of nine essential habits.

The book's first habit focuses on creating a clear and compelling vision. Successful

9 Habits of Thriving Sole Proprietors: Mastering Success in Your Own Venture.

108

sole entrepreneurs realize the value of having a clear purpose and long-term objectives for their organizations. This vision acts as a guiding star, providing guidance and determination to overcome obstacles.

The second habit, which builds on this foundation, emphasizes excellent time management. To maximize efficiency, thriving solo owners are skilled at prioritizing work and delegating duties. They can focus on high-impact activities that generate growth by effectively managing their time.

The third habit discusses the importance of lifelong learning and

9 Habits of Thriving Sole Proprietors: Mastering Success in Your Own Venture.

109

self-improvement. Successful solo entrepreneurs commit to continuing education and skill growth in an ever-changing business world. This practice keeps them adaptive and ready to seize new possibilities.

The fourth habit emphasizes the importance of networking and relationship building. Successful sole entrepreneurs realize the importance of connections in business success. They build a strong network of connections, partners, and mentors to gain access to vital resources and insights.

Following that, the fifth habit is financial caution. Thriving solo entrepreneurs

9 Habits of Thriving Sole Proprietors: Mastering Success in Your Own Venture.

110

prioritize financial stability by carefully controlling spending, making prudent investments, and maintaining a strong cash flow. This practice ensures that their businesses stay resilient even in difficult economic times.

The sixth habit emphasizes the significance of invention and creativity. Successful solo owners are always looking for new methods to innovate and separate themselves from their competitors. This practise enables them to stay ahead of the competition and provide distinct value to their clients.

The seventh habit delves into the importance of effective communication.

9 Habits of Thriving Sole Proprietors: Mastering Success in Your Own Venture.

111

Successful sole entrepreneurs are excellent at communicating their vision, beliefs, and offerings to diverse stakeholders like customers, workers, and partners. Transparent communication builds trust and strengthens corporate partnerships.

Adaptability and resilience are the focus of the eighth habit. Successful lone proprietors demonstrate a great ability to adapt and persevere in the face of setbacks and uncertainties. This habit enables them to handle setbacks and pivot as needed without losing sight of their long-term objectives.

9 Habits of Thriving Sole Proprietors: Mastering Success in Your Own Venture.

112

Finally, the ninth habit emphasizes a comprchcnsivc approach to well-being. Successful sole proprietors understand the significance of preserving physical, mental, and emotional wellness. They guarantee they have the energy and mindset required to sustain their enterprises over time by prioritizing self-care.

Finally, "9 Habits of Thriving Sole Proprietors: Mastering Success in Your Own Venture" provides a detailed summary of the important habits that drive sole proprietorship success. By adopting these practices, entrepreneurs can build resilient businesses that not only survive but thrive in the volatile

9 Habits of Thriving Sole Proprietors: Mastering Success in Your Own Venture.

113

entrepreneurial landscape. Individuals can prepare the way for long-term success in their entrepreneurial endeavors by combining strategic vision, effective time management, constant learning, relationship-building, financial prudence, innovation, communication, adaptability, and holistic well-being. This book provides prospective and current sole owners with the tools and insights they need to handle the obstacles and possibilities of the business world.

www.ingramcontent.com/pod-product-compliance
Lightning Source LLC
Chambersburg PA
CBHW062330290526
45794CB00005B/1982